THE

K I D'S

GUIDE TO
NEW YORK CITY

4th
edition

Eileen Ogintz

Globe
Pequot

Essex, Connecticut

Special thanks to my daughter Mel Yemma and Nora Brown, who was raised in Brooklyn, for their research help. Thanks to the staff at NYC museums and NYCgo.com. Thanks also to the NYC kids at the American Museum of Natural History's Lang Science Program for their insights and to CityPASS for the passes that facilitated research.

All the information in this guidebook is subject to change. We recommend that you call ahead to obtain current information before traveling.

Globe Pequot

An imprint of Globe Pequot, the trade division of
The Rowman & Littlefield Publishing Group, Inc.
4501 Forbes Blvd., Ste. 200
Lanham, MD 20706
www.rowman.com

Distributed by NATIONAL BOOK NETWORK

British Library Cataloguing in Publication Information Available

Library of Congress Cataloging-in-Publication Data Available

ISBN 9781493070442 (paperback)
ISBN 9781493070459 (epub)

∞™ The paper used in this publication meets the minimum requirements of American National Standard for Information Sciences—Permanence of Paper for Printed Library Materials, ANSI/NISO Z39.48-1992.

Contents

1

Say Hello to the Big Apple!

Ready to take a big bite out of the Big Apple?

There is so much to do here that you are guaranteed to have fun—sports, art, science, music, theater, and more! You can also take your pick of any food. And it will be great.

Check out all the big buildings. This is one place you won't get bored. In fact, there's so much to do it's impossible to do it all no matter how long you stay.

That's why New York is always tops on kids' lists of places they want to visit. Listen to all the different languages that people are speaking. The experts say more than 600 different ones, everything from Arabic to Spanish to Chinese, Russian, and Hebrew. But New York is also

A NYC KID SAYS:
"I've got friends who are Chinese, Korean, Puerto Rican, Mexican, Black, Jewish, Indian . . . and a lot of others, too."
—Regan, 11, NYC

{ **What's Cool?** You can always find something to eat—right on the street. New York kids love soft pretzels from the street vendors. You'll also see vendors and trucks selling kabobs, ice cream, cupcakes, and Italian ice. Visit nyfta.org and take your pick . . .

How Did New York Get Its Name?

The Algonquin Indians and other tribes were the first New Yorkers, here when Henry Hudson showed up in 1609. He was actually looking for a passageway to the Orient when he stumbled into New York Harbor. Fifteen years later, the Dutch had settled here and named the area New Amsterdam. But by 1674, the English were in charge, and they renamed the busy settlement New York after James, Duke of York.

A NYC KID SAYS:
"One of my favorite NYC souvenirs is the subway shirt. You can buy them for a friend with the letter of their name!"
—Brian, 12, NYC

DID YOU KNOW?

Manhattan is an island just over 12 miles long and 2.5 miles wide.

NYC is shaped kind of like a fish, and to get on or off most of it, you've got to use either a bridge or a tunnel.

home to millions of parents and kids. Many of them have come from around the world to live here. No matter what they wear or what language they speak, they're all still New Yorkers.

What's Cool? You might be able to be on TV if you get up really early and hold up a funny sign outside a broadcasting studio. Head to NBC's Studios at Rockefeller Center (just off Fifth Avenue between 49th and 50th Streets) to join the crowd at *The Today Show*. You can join the crowd at *Good Morning America* in Times Square. There are other shows filmed in NYC too. The website nytix.com can tell you how to get tickets.

Ask a New York kid on his way to school or in a museum to point you to the nearest playground or place to get a bagel.

A VISITING KID SAYS:
"I was really surprised how easy it is to get around on subways and buses!"
—Jake, 9, Aspen, CO

So where do you want to go first? *The Kid's Guide to New York City* helps you have the most fun! We've asked

DID YOU KNOW?

New York City is made up of five different boroughs: Manhattan, Brooklyn, Queens, the Bronx, and Staten Island. Nearly 8.5 million people live here—that's nearly double the number of people who live in the whole state of Colorado.

kids to help, too. You'll see their ideas in every chapter.

GOT A MAP?

Manhattan is split into the East Side and the West Side by Fifth Avenue. You'll hear people talk about the Upper East Side and Upper West Side as if they were different countries! A lot of kids also live in Brooklyn, the Bronx, Staten Island, and Queens. It's easier to understand New York if you think of it as a lot of little neighborhoods. You'll also hear some other funny names of neighborhoods, and if you know what they mean, you're on your way to becoming a New Yorker!

Pick places within one neighborhood to explore at one time. Your feet won't get nearly so tired!

SUBWAYS & BUSES

Got comfy shoes? The best way to get around NYC is on foot—or on public transportation. Subways are the quickest—the first subway car is always the most fun—but you can see where you're going on the bus. Make sure you've

What's Cool? Look at all the amazing architecture in New York! Draw a picture of your favorite building.

TELL THE ADULTS:

- **MTA Bus Time** (bustime.mta.info) shows you the location of the next bus.

- **NYCGO.com** is the place to find out where to go, stay, eat and what's going on when you visit. Timeout.com is another good resource as is MommyPoppins.com.

- **The Citymapper app** (https://citymapper.com/nyc) tells you which subway or bus to ride. It lets you know when the next bus or train is due to arrive, and the cost.

got a yellow **MetroCard** to pay for your ride, or you can tap and use your own contactless card or phone with the MTA's OMNY system (omny.info). Check out the big subway maps that are posted in every train station. Download the MYMTA app (mymta.info) that includes trains, subways, busses, the Staten Island Ferry, NYC Ferry Service, PATH, and New Jersey Transit. The app also enables you to plan accessible trips for those with mobility challenges. Check out the tile walls along some of the platforms—they're often the work of local artists.

DID YOU KNOW?

To hail a taxi, tell your parents to stand next to the curb and wave really hard. Don't forget to buckle your seatbelt when you get inside. These days, if you call an Uber, you may get a Yellow Taxi.

The Dutch bought Manhattan Island from Native Americans in 1626 for about $24 worth of tools and necklaces. See what you can buy in NYC today for $24.

TELL THE ADULTS:

- Leave lots of time to explore the city's neighborhoods as well as museums! That's where you'll discover the real New York—from coffee shops and delis to playgrounds and firehouses. Stop by a firehouse. New York firefighters will be glad to show you around—if they're not off fighting a fire!

- Make sure each member of the family picks out where you're going and what you're doing each day.

- NY Metro Parents (www.nymetroparents.com) is a good resource to find out special happenings at the time you are in the city.

A VISITING KID SAYS:
"My favorite thing to do in NYC is travel around the city and window-shop."
—Brendan, 13, ME

2

New York City's
Neighborhoods

Get your sneakers on!

The best way to see the way kids live in New York is to walk around the city's neighborhoods. And you'll want to wear your comfiest shoes.

Ask kids you see to point you to their favorite playground or pizza place in the neighborhood. They'll know—just like you would at home.

A VISITING KID SAYS:
"The subway went so fast!"
—Gina, 8, Naples, Italy

Even if you get to stroll through just one or two city neighborhoods, you'll realize New York is a lot more than skyscrapers, restaurants, and big stores. **Big Apple Greeter** (www .bigapplegreeter.org) is an organization of volunteers that give visitors free tours of different areas of New York City. Ask for a kid-friendly tour!

- **Alphabet City** is named for avenues A, B, C, and D.

- **Chelsea** was named after a fancy neighborhood in London.

- **Chinatown** has become the biggest Asian community in North America. As many as 100,000 people live here!

- **Flatiron District** is named after the building on Broadway and 23rd Street whose top looks like an old-fashioned iron.

DID YOU KNOW?

The **ferry to Staten Island** is free, and it's a great way to take in the view of the NYC skyline. Check out siferry.com for the schedule.

- **Greenwich Village** started out as a 17th-century suburb, a green village. Today it's full of people, cafes, clubs, shops, and New York University.

- **Ground Zero** is the area of Lower Manhattan destroyed in 2001. One World Trade Center, formerly Freedom Tower, is the main building of the rebuilt World Trade Center. Across the street, the National September 11 Memorial was opened to the public on September 12, 2011. There are special activity stations for kids at the 9/11 Memorial Museum (180 Greenwich St.; 212-312-8800; 911memorial.org).

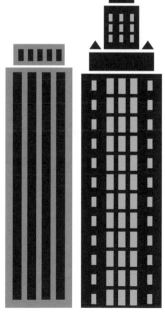

- **Harlem** is north of 110th Street and has long been a hub of New York's Black community. The neighborhood has changed rapidly and is home to cafes, clubs, and Columbia University.

- **Little Italy,** once home to many Italian Americans, is the site of some great Italian restaurants.

- **Lower East Side** was once the center of Jewish life in New York, now is known for its stores, hip restaurants, and shopping deals.

- **Midtown** is just what it sounds like—the middle of town where there are lots of skyscrapers, restaurants, businesses, and stores.

- **Nolita** means "North of Little Italy" and that's where this trendy neighborhood is located.

- **SoHo** means South of Houston Street. (New Yorkers pronounce it "HOW-ston.") It has lots of art galleries and stores. You might want to stop in at the **New York City Fire Museum** (278 Spring St.; 212-691-1303;

DID YOU KNOW?

2.5 million people live on Brooklyn—nearly a million more than live on Manhattan Island.

nycfiremuseum.org) while you're in the neighborhood to see how New York firefighters have always done their jobs and the old hand-pulled and horse-drawn engines they used in the old days. It's housed in a 1904 firehouse.

> **A NYC KID SAYS:**
> "Every kid who visits NYC should not miss Brooklyn Bridge Park—it's one of the coolest parks I've ever been to. It's super cool to see and play volleyball at and rollerblade for free!"
> —Josh, 10, Brooklyn

DID YOU KNOW?

You can walk or bike from Manhattan to Brooklyn across the **Brooklyn Bridge**. It's about a mile. The bridge took 16 years to build in the late 1800s. DUMBO, the Brooklyn neighborhood named for Down Under the Manhattan Bridge Overpass, has one of the city's best views, as well as a park, a carousel, a ferry pier, very cool shops, cafes, theaters, and the original Grimaldi's Pizza.

- **Times Square** at 42nd Street and Broadway is the heart of the theater district—and where you'll find the most souvenir shops.

- **TriBeCa,** on the Lower West Side, is short for "Triangle Below Canal (Street)."

- **Upper East Side** (North of 59th Street and east of Central Park) has some of New York's fanciest apartment buildings as well as a lot of shopping at stores such as Bloomingdale's.

- **Upper West Side** (North of 59th Street and everything west of Central Park) is the area that includes the American Museum of Natural History, a kids' favorite.

Brooklyn and Beyond

Young hipsters-to-be will want to head to Williamsburg, in Brooklyn. But there's plenty else for families here, including:

- **Coney Island**, where New Yorkers have been coming for more than a century for fun, including the wooden Cyclone rollercoaster, the Phoenix family thrill coaster, a Sky Chaser ropes course, the beach boardwalk, the Abe Stark Skating Arena, B&B Carousel, and the New York Aquarium. It's also where the Brooklyn Cyclones play minor league baseball. Fireworks shoot off on Friday nights in the summer! (Surf Avenue and Stillwell Avenue, Brooklyn, NY 11224; coneyislandfunguide.com).

- **The Brooklyn Children's Museum**, with daily special programs as well as plenty of free fun exhibits (145 Brooklyn Ave., Brooklyn, NY 11213; 718-735-4400; brooklynkids.org/visit).

- **The Brooklyn Botanic Garden**, with its discovery garden designed for young naturalists with hands-on experiences in a meadow, marsh, vegetable garden, and more. In the summer there are special Kids' Discovery Stations and nature projects to do at home (several entrances, including 455 Flatbush Ave., Brooklyn, NY 11225; 718-623-7200; bbg.org).

- **The Barclays Center** is the multipurpose arena where the NBA's Brooklyn Nets and the New York Islanders NHL team play (620 Atlantic Ave., Brooklyn, NY 11217; barclayscenter.com).

- **Prospect Park**, in the heart of Brooklyn with outdoor summer concerts, birdwatching, the Prospect Park Zoo, boating, biking, greenmarket, playgrounds, the Audubon Center, carousel, and the innovative play area—the Zucker Natural Exploration Area (95 Prospect Park West, Brooklyn, NY 11215; 718-965-8951; prospectpark.org).

- **The Brooklyn Museum**, New York's second largest, with a collection of 1.5 million works from ancient Egyptian masterpieces to contemporary art, and special "Family Art Magic" programs on Sundays for young kids 4-6 and other classes for those 6-13 (200 Eastern Pkwy., Brooklyn, NY 11238; 718-638-5000; brooklynmuseum.org).

A lot of kids who visit New York also like to head downtown, especially to eat, shop, and people-watch. Many families live downtown, too.

Greenwich Village—a lot of people just call it "The Village"—has lots of little stores, cafes, and parks, as well as New York University. You'll see a lot of students in Washington Square Park and parents with kids who live in the neighborhood.

If you love sports, head toward the Hudson River, and in between 17th and 23rd Streets you'll find the **Chelsea Piers Sports and Entertainment Complex** (chelseapiers.com). The complex is on four different historic piers over the river, and you can take your pick from

DID YOU KNOW?

The Bronx is the only one of New York's five boroughs connected to the mainland. To get to Manhattan, Queens, Staten Island, or Brooklyn, you have to take a tunnel or a bridge.

Most NYC neighborhoods are only about 10 square blocks. They've got ice cream shops, pizza parlors, parks, schools, and lots of families and pets.

For some kids, their apartment building is like your block at home. They play with kids in their building and make friends with the doorman whose job it is to keep track of who goes in and out. They also go trick-or-treating in their building on Halloween!

17 different sports to play, from rock climbing to ice-skating to sailing to soccer and more!

Very close to the piers is the **High Line** (thehighline.org), a 1.45 mile-long elevated park built on top of old New York City freight train tracks. The park runs from Gansevoort Street in the Meatpacking District to West 34th Street, between 10th and 12th Avenues. You'll find restaurants, places to get ice cream, and public art. Download the High Line app (thehighline.org) or get a free pocket guide from the website.

Head south of the Village for more shopping and eating in SoHo, Little Italy, Chinatown, and the Lower East Side, once the biggest Jewish community in the world that today has lots of hip shops and restaurants.

Many kids move to New York every year from other countries with their families—from Asia, Africa, India, the Caribbean Islands, and Central America, among other places. They're part of what makes New York so great.

{ **What's Cool?** The Diller-Von Furstenberg Sundeck and Water Feature at the High Line (between 14th Street and 15th Street. When the High Line was an empty railroad track, water accumulated here naturally. The designers planned this water feature where kids and adults can dip their toes in the warmer months. Visit thehighline.org for more details and other fun places.

The Bronx Zoo

Ready to get up close and personal with the animals?

At the Bronx Zoo (2300 Southern Blvd., Bronx, NY 10460; 718-220-5100; bronxzoo.com), take your pick.

You can head to the African rain forest and visit more than 20 gorillas in the Congo Gorilla Forest. Maybe you'd rather meet Siberian tigers at Tiger Mountain. In the summer, you can wander amid 1,000 different kinds of butterflies and moths. Check out a black leopard in JungleWorld, an endangered snow leopard in the Himalayan habitat, or see all the little rodents in the Mouse House. Take the Bengali Express Monorail through Wild Asia, past tigers, elephants, rhinos, antelopes, and more.

There's a lot of ground to cover, and you won't want to miss anything. There is a Zoo Shuttle you can take from one part of the zoo to another and a Skyfari gondola that gets you from Asia to the Children's Zoo in no time.

A VISITING KID SAYS:
"Don't worry about transportation. It's really easy to get around. I was surprised!"
—Jake, 9, Aspen, CO

At the Children's Zoo, open April through October, kids can climb into child-size heron nests, walk through a prairie dog tunnel, or climb a 20-foot spider web made of rope. In the forest, climb up the platform 14 feet high to get face-to-face with a porcupine or look through a telescope. Remember to stop and feed the goats.

For more than 100 years, this zoo has been welcoming kids and parents. It's also a center for conservation and part of the Wildlife Conservation Society, which manages the world's largest network of urban wildlife parks including the Central Park Zoo, Queens Zoo, and New York Aquarium as well as the Bronx Zoo. Check out wcs.org.

What's your favorite animal?

What's Cool? There are hundreds of baby animals born every year at the Bronx Zoo.

TELL THE ADULTS:

- FREE IS GOOD! Many city museums have free admission nights and free family guides. Check their websites before visiting.

- **Big Apple Greeter** (212-669-8159; bigapplegreeter .org) offers FREE tours to visiting families and gives you all their top picks in their favorite neighborhoods. You need to make an appointment several weeks in advance.

- **NYC Parks** (nycgovparks.org), including the Brooklyn Bridge Park (brooklynbridgepark) on the water-front, which has become a mecca for families since it opened, complete with bike trails, playgrounds, sand volleyball courts, and even a beach.

- For budding fashionistas, the **Fashion Institute of Technology Museum** features rotating exhibits by students and a gallery of fashion, dating back to the 18th century (fitnyc.edu/museum.asp; Seventh Avenue and 27th Street; 212-217-4558).

- The **National Museum of the American Indian—New York**, the George Gustav Heye Center, has exhibits, daily hands-on activities, and a performing arts center (Alexander Hamilton U.S. Custom House, One Bowling

Green, New York, NY 10004; 212-514-3700; nmai.si.edu/explore/forfamilies).

- The **New York Public Library** (42nd Street and Fifth Avenue), where there is a Children's Center with ongoing programs for families, including storytelling and guest appearances by authors.

- The **Schomburg Center for Research in Black Culture**, part of the city's library center, has the largest collection of everything from documents to art to recordings related to the Black experience (515 Malcolm X Blvd., New York, NY 10037; 917-275-6975; nypl.org/locations/schomburg).

- Kayak for free in the summer from the **Downtown Boathouse** at several locations including Pier 96 (56th Street in Hudson River Park) and 72nd Street, north of Pier I cafe in Riverside Park (downtown boathouse.org/free-kayaking/).

- The **Federal Reserve Bank of New York**, where you can see the gold vault, the world's largest accumulation of gold—as long as you reserve a guided tour in advance (33 Liberty St., New York, NY 10045; 212-720-6130; newyorkfed.org/aboutthefed/visiting.html).

Stories Everywhere!

There are NYC libraries (nypl.org) all over the city, and in them you'll find many stories that take place in New York. Do you have a favorite? Here are some that NYC librarians think you'd like:

The Adventures of Taxi Dog by Debra and Sal Barracca, the tale of a dog's adoption by a taxi driver and the fun experiences they have from the front seat.

Eloise by Kay Thompson tells the story of a six-year-old who grows up in the Plaza Hotel.

Lyle, Lyle Crocodile by Bernard Waber is about a NYC family who finds a crocodile named Lyle in their bathtub!

The Cricket in Times Square by George Selden follows the adventures of a cricket who ends up in Times Square.

Stuart Little by E.B. White is the story of a NYC family's little mouse and takes place all around Central Park.

Harriet the Spy by Louise Fitzhugh follows the adventures of a sixth-grader who lives in Manhattan.

From the Mixed-up Files of Mrs. Basil E. Frankweiler by E.L. Konigsburg tells the story of two Connecticut kids who camp out in the Metropolitan Museum and solve a mystery.

What's your favorite book set in New York?

_____

_____

_____

_____

Movies Everywhere!

Lots of movies and TV shows are set in NYC, and many are filmed here. Just a few of them include:

Lyle, Lyle Crocodile
Spider-Man
Superman
Batman
Home Alone 2
Ghostbusters
Stuart Little
The Secret Life of Pets
School of Rock
West Side Story
Annie
Night at the Museum movies

How many other New York–based movies can you name?

Harlem

More than a third of the length of Manhattan is north of 110th Street, and that includes Harlem. First settled in the 1600s by Dutch tobacco farmers, Harlem in the 1920s was the most famous Black community in the country, maybe in the world. It has become a hot neighborhood again with new stores, restaurants, and attractions. Think you want to be a star? The **Apollo Theater** at 253 West 125th St. in Harlem has started to hold "amateur nights" to find new stars (for more information, visit apollotheater.org). If you're a dancer, you might want to see a performance at the **Dance Theatre of Harlem** (466 West 152nd St.; 212-690-2800; dance theatreofharlem.org).

DID YOU KNOW?

The name **Manhattan** comes from a Native American word that means "the place of hills."

NYC's nickname, **The Big Apple**, came from a tourism campaign in 1971, and it has stuck ever since.

The Bronx Zoo is the largest youth employer in the Bronx, helping to transform lives in an underserved community.

A NYC KID SAYS:
"Go to the parks. They are always relaxing!"
—Sam, 13, NYC

WORD SEARCH

Find some of the neighborhoods and boroughs of NYC.
(Words are horizontal, vertical, and diagonal.)

Brooklyn
Chinatown
Greenwich
 Village
Ground Zero
Harlem

Little Italy
Lower East Side
Manhattan
Midtown
Queens
SoHo

Staten Island
The Bronx
Times Square
TriBeCa

```
S T S M U X O M D S D X Y R J E N
T I O A A H E M S N T L W K G T B
A M T N J L S G P Y A B Z A D H R
T E G H R V O W F T V L L W J E O
E S K A Q T H P I W R L S N Z B O
N S H T Z M O E E J I B D I O R K
I Q I T J H L S F V X Y N S N O L
S U E A Z T L R H H R L X R T N Y
L A V N T E K C Z V T G H L R X N
A R E I W K I G R O U N D Z E R O
N E L E X W Z E A F O H R N N X J
D M R E N E D I S M I D T O W N Q
H I H E M C H I N A T O W N E Q U
C T E V L O W E R E A S T S I D E
G R N T R C L W T X N V U H Q W E
G K T D T R I B E C A Q I M X O N
U N S P U O D W K B R N S F B R S
```

See page 145 for the answer key.

3

Mummies, Knights
& All Kinds of Art

Name the place in New York

where you can time travel from ancient Egypt to Japan, from Europe hundreds of years ago to the US today.

Stumped? The answer is the **Metropolitan Museum of Art** (Fifth Avenue and 82nd Street; 212-535-7710; metmuseum.org). It's so big that from end to end, the museum stretches four New York City blocks—a quarter of a mile! There are more than 90 bathrooms!

The Met, as New Yorkers call it, has been around for more than 130 years. When you walk in the enormous front doors, you're entering one of the biggest and best art museums in the world. And even if you think you hate museums, this one can be fun as long as you know where to go. Of course, you can't possibly see everything in one visit!

DID YOU KNOW?

The **Brooklyn Children's Museum** (145 Brooklyn Ave., Brooklyn, NY; 718-735-4400; brooklynkids.org) was the first museum created just for kids. That was in 1899, and since then hundreds of children's museums have opened around the world. There is also a **Children's Museum of Manhattan** (212 W. 83rd St.; 212-721-1223; cmom.org).

Ready to hop in a time machine? You'll find it on #MetKids, the museum's website made for, with, and by kids (metmuseum.org/art/online-features/metkids). The Met has special family guides to the museum that you can download from its website, metmuseum.org, or you can pick them up at the information desk when you arrive.

And when you get tired, you can run and play all you want in Central Park just outside. Maybe snack on a pretzel from a street vendor!

A lot of kids head for the ancient Egyptian Temple of Dendur first. In fact, it's one of the most popular exhibits in the entire museum. The temple, built in 15 BC, was taken apart in Egypt and transported by ship to New York. Engineers had to make detailed drawings so they would know how to put it back together to match how it appeared on the banks of the Nile River. If it had not been moved, it would have been covered by waters rising behind a new dam that was being built. The government of Egypt was very happy the temple could be brought to New York and gave it to our government as a present. The Met built an entire area to house the temple.

Kids also like to see the mummies that are in galleries in the main building near the Temple of Dendur. Thirteen of the mummies contain bodies, twelve of them adults and one child. We know that because museum experts did scans—similar to X-rays—of the mummies.

Have you ever imagined being a Knight in Shining Armor, fighting battles with a big sword? You might not want to after you stop to see the Met's collection of Arms and Armor. Those suits were heavy! So were the weapons!

Kids especially like the Costume Institute. You can see the kind of clothes people wore in different countries and a long time ago.

Of course, you're not going to leave without seeing some paintings and sculptures. Take your pick—

TELL THE ADULTS

Visiting an art museum can be a real adventure! Many NYC museums like the Metropolitan offer special family workshops for kids of different ages, exhibit guides, and apps for touring particular exhibits. There are also special programs for kids with special challenges. For example, the Met offers Drop-In Drawing the 1st and 3d Friday of each month from 6:30 to 8:30 p.m.; the 2nd Saturday and Sunday of each month, there are "How Did They Do That?" 30-minute workshops from 1 to 4 p.m. to show you how works of art were created.

impressionist art from France, sculptures from the US, African masks, or Chinese porcelain. What part of the world do you want to visit today?

Museum educators offer these tips to make any art museum more fun:

- Look closely at the art and encourage the kids to imagine the sights, sounds, and smells you would experience if you stepped inside.

- Strike a pose like a sculpture.

- Seek out artworks that portray kids.

- Create a theme. Search for faces, crowns, animals, or shapes.

- Bring along sketch pads and let the kids sketch what they see.

> A NYC KIDS SAYS:
> "My favorite NYC museum is the Museum of the Moving Image because there's so many hands-on exhibits, and you can make your own stop motion clip."
> —Marion, 12, NYC

- Play "I Spy" in one gallery.

- Pick two different works of art and compare how they are similar and different.

- Leave when the kids—and you—have had enough, but keep the art conversation going. What was everyone's favorite?

Doughnut or Snail?

A lot of people thought the **Guggenheim Museum** (1071 Fifth Ave.; 212-355-4965; guggenheim.org) was a weird building when it was built. Some people thought it looked like a snail, others a doughnut. The building was designed as a spiral by famed architect Frank Lloyd Wright, with the art hung on the walls alongside a ramp. You may think some of these paintings are weird. Take the elevator to the top and look at the art as you head down the ramp.

    The Cloisters (Fort Tryon Park at 193rd Street; 212-923-3700; metmuseum.org/visit/visit-the-cloisters) was put together from parts of buildings that date back to the 15th century! They were brought from Europe. Kids like to come to this branch of the Metropolitan Museum overlooking the Hudson River because they can play in the gardens and check out the brave knights and ferocious dragons on view. Don't miss the seven gigantic Unicorn Tapestries that were woven around 1500. How many plants can you count? There are images of more than 100.

The **Museum of Modern Art**
(11 W. 53rd St.; 212-708-9400; moma.org) is a great place to
see some masterpieces you've seen in school like Van Gogh's
The Starry Night, Picasso's *Les Demoiselles d'Avignon*, and Rodin's
great sculpture. Check out all the exhibits of appliances and
even sports cars as well as the Sculpture Garden. See
sculptures so big they had to be installed with a crane!

Love history? Check out the **Museum of the City of
New York** (1220 Fifth Ave.; 212-534-1672; mcny.org), where
you'll especially like the exhibit of toys and dolls owned by
NYC kids and the New York Historical Society DiMenna
Children's History Museum, where you learn something about
NYC history through the eyes of kids who lived here at
different times in history (170 Central Park West at Richard
Gilder Way [77th Street], New York, NY 10024; 212-873-3400;
nyhistory.org). Find activities you can do at home too.

DID YOU KNOW:

There is a really fun museum in NYC that is all about math—
the **National Museum of Mathematics**. Even if you don't like
math, you'll love all the interactive activities here. Check out
what you can do at momath.org and see what you can do online
(11 East 26th Street NYC, NY 10010; 212-542-0566).

4

Dinosaurs, Fighter Jets & Outer Space

THINK DINOSAURS. LOTS OF THEM!

The **American Museum of Natural History** (Central Park West at 79th Street; 212-769-5100; amnh.org) is home to one of the largest collections of vertebrate fossils—nearly one million in all!

This museum is the first one that many New York kids come to, and they return again and again. It's been here for more than 150 years, and, like the Met, it's so huge you can't possibly see everything all at once. There are 23 buildings and more than 40 exhibition halls. Head to the fourth floor to see the dinosaurs. Say "hi" to the T. rex, apatosaurus, stegosaurus, and triceratops. Make sure to see the dinosaur nest.

Kids also like to see the huge dioramas in the mammal halls on the first, second, and third floors that show you

DID YOU KNOW?

The **American Museum of Natural History** has a special website just for kids with activities and fun facts about science and the exhibits you can see at the museum. To find out about fossils, share discoveries with the scientists who made them, and more, visit amnh.org/explore/ology.

the animals in their native habitats—they've got Alaskan brown bear, African elephants, water buffaloes from Asia, plus many others!

You'll probably also want to see the giant 94-foot model of a blue whale. She weighs 21,000 pounds! You can find it on the first floor in the Milstein Hall of Ocean Life, and when you get there, you'll be staring at the biggest model of the biggest creature that ever lived on earth.

For ocean lovers, there are lots of other dioramas— of sea lions, dolphins, flying fish, and more. You can find activities about the living oceans on the museum's website, amnh.org.

If you like rocks, you'll love the all-new Mignone Halls of Gems and Minerals that tell the fascinating story of how the vast diversity of mineral species arose on our planet, how scientists classify and study them, and how we use them for personal adornment, tools, and technology. The galleries feature more than 5,000 specimens from 98 countries. Make sure to stop and look at the Star of India. It's the world's biggest blue star sapphire.

{ **What's Cool?** See the real exhibits behind the characters featured in the *Night at the Museum* movies at the American Museum of Natural History on the self-guided tour: amnh.org/plan-your-visit/self-guided-tours/night-at-the-museum-tour. There are other special tours, including the Dino Tour.

The Hayden Planetarium at the museum is really cool too. You'll feel like you're in a spaceship at the Space Theater! It's all part of the big seven-floor Rose Center for Earth and Space. Follow the Cosmic Pathway through 13 billion years; don't miss the chance to see the latest news from space and rock samples and models from around the world.

The museum's Hall of Biodiversity is the place to go to see why we should all care about the environment and how to protect all different kinds of life. This is where you can visit a diorama of a rain forest from Central Africa. It stretches for 90 feet, and you can step inside to see what happens to a rain forest when people don't take care of it. See all the leaves? There are more than 500,000 here, each made by hand! How about all the bugs?

If you're visiting around the holidays, you'll love the Origami Holiday Tree decorated with fanciful Japanese origami ornaments.

Check off what you saw at the American Museum of Natural History:

❏ T. rex

❏ A brown bear

❏ Fragments of the Cape York meteorite

❏ A rain forest

❏ A giant squid

❏ The blue whale, the world's largest animal

❏ A butterfly

❏ The planets of our solar system

❏ The Hayden Sphere

❏ A gem

❏ An elephant seal

Transforming the Experience

Did you stop at the Northwest Hall? It was the museum's oldest gallery. Now after a major rennovation with the help of leaders from Indigenous Pacific Northwest Coast Communities, they've worked hard over several years to highlight Native Northwest Coast Life for museum visitors. There are more than 1,000 items in this collection! Were you able to see the giant canoe?

The new Gilder Center for Science, Education, and Innovation is designed to transform your visit from the spectacular architecture to the connection of many of the museum's buildings—across four city blocks—and special learning zones. As large as a hockey rink, with walls 23 feet high, the Clearing will surround visitors with projections of nature at all scales while the Davis Family Butterfly Vivarium will surround visitors with live free-flying butterflies at all times of the year. Don't miss the Susan and Peter J. Solomon Family Insectarium—even if you hate bugs. Check out the leafcutter ants and the huge bee hive. Hear the music? That's Central Park's insects!

A VISITING KID SAYS:
"The Intrepid Museum is my favorite museum in New York. Kids should get a small model of the *Intrepid* as a souvenir."
—Jake, 12, Weston, CT

Fighter Jets, Submarines, and Space Ships

Have you ever set foot on a giant aircraft carrier? Welcome to the **Intrepid Sea, Air & Space Museum** that is on the aircraft carrier *Intrepid*. More than 50,000 men served on board, starting during World War II.

Get a close-up look at the restored aircraft. It was hard to take off and land in the middle of the ocean! See where the sailors lived. Really tight quarters! Want to have a sleepover here?

This museum (Pier 86, W. 46th Street and 12th Avenue, New York, NY 10036; 212-245-0072; intrepidmuseum.org) is also the place to see the space shuttle *Enterprise*, the prototype NASA orbiter that paved the way for the space shuttle programs. Before you visit, you might want to download the museum's free iPhone app Mission Intrepid: Explore Enterprise.

Walk underneath and see how big it is! Check out the Russian Soyuz TMA-6 space capsule. How are they different?

Climb aboard the *USS Growler*, a guided missile submarine, and see the once top-secret missile command center. Do you think you'd like living aboard a sub?

Do you like to go really fast? The British Airways Concorde did in her day, crossing the Atlantic in less than three hours—supersonic speed!

Kid-Friendly Museum Events

There are some 150 museums in New York City. Many have special programs online and in person for kids and families. See which ones you might want to visit at nycgo.com/museums-and-galleries. Here are the websites for some of the museums kids most like to visit in NYC.

American Folk Art Museum: 2 Lincoln Square; (212) 595-9533; folkartmuseum.org.

American Museum of Natural History: Central Park West at 79th Street; (212) 769-5100; amnh.org.

Brooklyn Children's Museum: 145 Brooklyn Ave., Brooklyn; (718) 735-4400; brooklynkids.org.

Brooklyn Museum: 200 Eastern Pkwy., Brooklyn; (718) 638-5000; brooklynmuseum.org.

Children's Museum of Manhattan: 212 W. 83rd St.; (212) 721-1223; cmom.org.

El Museo del Barrio about Latino culture: 1230 Fifth Ave.; (212) 831-7272; elmuseo.org.

Guggenheim Museum: 1071 Fifth Ave.; (212) 423-3500; guggenheim.org.

Intrepid Sea, Air & Space Museum: Pier 86, W. 46th St. and 12th Avenue; (212) 245-0072; intrepidmuseum.org.

Lower East Side Tenement Museum: 103 Orchard St.; (212) 982-8420; tenement.org.

Metropolitan Museum of Art: 1000 Fifth Ave.; (212) 535-7710; metmuseum.org.

Museum of Arts and Design: 2 Columbus Circle; (212) 299-7777; madmuseum.org.

Museum of Broadway: 145 W. 45th St.; themuseumofbroadway.com

Museum of Illusions: 77 8th Ave.; (212) 645-3230; newyork.museumofillusions.us

Museum of Modern Art: 11 W. 53rd St.; (212) 708-9400; moma.org.

The Paley Center for Media (formerly the Museum of Television & Radio): 25 W. 52nd St.; (212) 621-6600; paleycenter.org.

Museum of the City of New York: 1220 Fifth Ave.; (212) 534-1672; mcny.org.

Museum of the Moving Image in Queens: 36-01 35th Ave.; (718) 777-6888; movingimage.us.

National Museum of the American Indian: Alexander Hamilton U.S. Custom House, One Bowling Green; (212) 514-3700; nmai.si.edu.

New Museum: 235 Bowery; (212) 219-1222; newmuseum.org.

NYC's Jewish Museum: 1109 Fifth Ave. (at 92nd St.); (212) 423-3200; jewishmuseum.org.

TELL THE ADULTS:

- The **American Museum of Natural History** is one of New York's top tourist attractions. If you are planning to visit here as well as other top attractions, CityPASS (citypass.com) can save you on admission and help you avoid lines.

- Be prepared for crowds! Come well fed and wear comfortable shoes!

- Divide and conquer if the kids are interested in different exhibits. A good resource for what the museum offers families is amnh.org/learn-teach/families.

- The American Museum of Natural History has a special website for kids: "ology" (amnh.org/explore/ology) and both virtual and in-person family programs. Download the free explorer app for a deeper dive in the exhibits and directions in where to find what you want to see.

- Astronomy Live programs at the Hayden Planetarium offer interactive tours of the universe and views of the changing night sky.

- Leave time at the end for the gift shops—including the ones tied to special exhibitions. The American Museum of Natural History has cool stuff for kids!

DID YOU KNOW?

The **American Museum of Natural History** has more than 34 million objects and specimens. The **Metropolitan Museum of Art** has more than 2 million objects in its collections. But not everything is on view at once. Both museums are on every family's top to-do list when they visit NYC. That's why there are more visitors from out of town here than New Yorkers. More people visit the two museums than live in most American cities.

5
PLAY BALL!

Anywhere you go in the city,

you're bound to see someone wearing a Yankees or Mets hat, a Knicks T-shirt, or maybe a Jets or Giants jersey.

New York City is home to millions of dedicated fans, whether the teams win or lose. There is also the chance to watch special sporting events such as college basketball tournaments, track and field championships, professional ice-skating, and even dog shows!

If you want to see a New York sporting event, **Madison Square Garden** (msg.com) is a great place to go. Located on Seventh Avenue between 31st and 32nd Streets, Madison Square Garden is the home of the **New York Knicks** basketball team (nba.com/knicks), **New York Rangers** hockey team (rangers.nhl.com), and the professional women's basketball team, **The New York Liberty** (wnba.com/liberty). The **New York Islanders** hockey team plays at the **UBS Arena** (2400 Hempstead Turnpike, Elimont, NY 11003). The **Brooklyn Nets** basketball team (nba.com/nets) plays at the **Barclays Center** in Brooklyn (620 Atlantic Ave., Brooklyn, NY 11217; 917-618-6100; barclayscenter.com).

A NYC KID SAYS:
"Make sure you go to a baseball game. Theys are always fun and full of energy. At Yankees games, during the 7th inning stretch, people come out and sing the YMCA song and it's fun to sing along."
—Sam, 13, NYC

50

DID YOU KNOW?

Madison Square Garden (msg.com) wasn't always in the building that it is now. In fact, the Garden had gone through three other buildings before it made Seventh Avenue and 31st Street its home. The first Garden was built in 1879, and it was only 29 feet tall! The current Garden was built in 1968 and is now one of the greatest places in New York to watch a show, concert, or any sort of sporting event.

Love tennis? Come in late August and early September for the **US Open Tennis Championship** (usopen.org) in Flushing Meadows.

Also, the MetLife Stadium in East Rutherford, New Jersey, is where two famous New York football teams, the **New York Giants** (giants.com) and the **New York Jets** (newyorkjets.com), play.

New York City has two great baseball stadiums, which are home to two great ball clubs. There is Citi Field in Flushing, Queens, where the **New York Mets** play (newyork.mets.mlb.com), and Yankee Stadium, home to those Bronx Bombers, the **New York Yankees** (newyork.yankees.mlb.com).

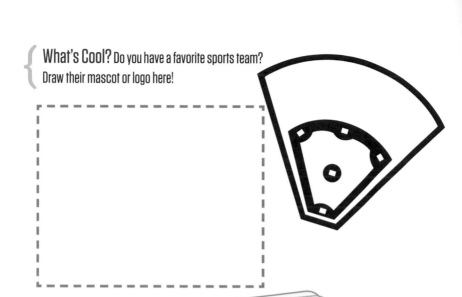

What's Cool? Do you have a favorite sports team? Draw their mascot or logo here!

DID YOU KNOW?

The **New York City Marathon**, always the first Sunday in November, is one of the world's biggest and most popular. Nearly two million people line the streets every fall to cheer on the more than 30,000 marathoners. The participants run 26.2 miles through all five boroughs, ending at Central Park.

There is a carousel and skatepark at **Pier 62** on the Hudson River (hudsonriverpark.org), part of a 9-acre park. There's also mini golf, basketball, trapeze, tennis, baseball, beach volleyball, public art, playgrounds, and kayaks and bikes for rent. You can pick up a bike at one place and drop it elsewhere with Citibike (citibikenyc.com).

If you go to a Mets or Yankees game, bring a mitt. Maybe you'll catch a fly ball out in the stands! And, your face may even be put up on the big screen TV where everyone can see you! If you want this to happen, it's helpful to wear plenty of team gear and show some spirit!

A VISITING KID SAYS:
"I think the Yankees are my favorite team now. I really like the game and how big the stadium is!"
—George, 9, Australia

DID YOU KNOW?

The **New York Yankees** (newyork.yankees.mlb.com) and **New York Mets** (newyork.mets.mlb.com) are playing in stadiums that were built next door to where they previously played. So are the **Giants** (giants.com) and the **Jets** (newyorkjets.com) of the National Football League—they are sharing the new MetLife Stadium in New Jersey.

TELL THE ADULTS:

- Finding tickets to a New York sporting event is not as hard as some may think—although it does depend on what game you want to see. If you want to get them online, ticketmaster.com is a very simple way to find tickets, and there are many other websites that you can try as well. Or, you can try calling or going to the box office at the arena or stadium that is holding the event you want to see. You can often buy tickets from people selling them outside the stadium—but be careful. The prices you pay outside the stadium may be unreasonably high, and you could be getting a counterfeit ticket.

- If you can't get tickets to see the Yankees or the Mets, try a minor league team like the **Brooklyn Cyclones** (brooklyncyclones.com) on Coney Island.

- Ice-skating is expensive and crowded at **Rockefeller Center Ice Rink** outside Rockefeller Center, but it is really fun too (W. 49th Street and Fifth Avenue; rockefellercenter.com/tour-and -explore/the-ice-skating-rink/). There is also ice-skating on the **Wollman Rink** in Central Park (830 5th Ave., New York, NY 10065; 212-744-0882).

DID YOU KNOW?

The walkway leading into the arena at **Madison Square Garden** is now known as the "Walk of Fame" and recognizes performers, athletes, announcers, and coaches who have all demonstrated amazing things throughout their career, including Patrick Ewing (who played for the Knicks), and Wayne Gretzky and Mark Messier (who both played for the Rangers).

All city marathons are modeled on the **New York City Marathon.** Every year the NYC Marathon Team for Kids—runners from around the world—raises money on behalf of New York Road Runners youth services to help NYC kids be more active.

The Red Sox have never forgiven the Yankees for stealing Babe Ruth, so whenever the two teams play, it's considered a grudge match.

The **New York Botanical Garden** has a special Adventure Garden where kids can run around (2900 Southern Blvd., Bronx, NY; 718-817-8700; nybg.org).

Shop Till You Drop

New York is famous around the world for shopping. Here are some places NYC kids say you should go to find things you might not be able to get elsewhere:

American Girl Place New York

Where you can have lunch or tea with your American Girl Doll and buy matching outfits. 75 Rockefeller Plaza, New York, NY 10019; (877) 247-5223.

M&Ms New York

You can design your customized M&Ms. 1600 Broadway New York, NY 10019; (212) 295-3850; mms.com/en-us/mms -store-new-york.

FAO Schwarz

The iconic toy store at 30 Rockefeller Plaza, New York, NY; (800) 326-8638.

NBA Store

The largest in-store collection of official NBA, WNBA, and NBA G League merchandise and the chance to customize your jersey! 545 Fifth Ave., New York, NY 10017; (212) 457-3120; store.nba.com/nyc-store.

Museum shops

Each museum's gift shop is the place to bring home something from an exhibit you really liked—a book, toy, T-shirt, magnet.

Exit 9 Gift Emporium

Exit 9, located in Brooklyn and Manhattan, sells build-your-own Empire State Buildings alongside lots of funny souvenirs. 51 Avenue A, New York, NY 10009; (212) 228-0145; shopexit9.com.

Memories of New York

Skip the crowds of Times Square and head to 23rd Street to find classic New York souvenirs—Empire State Building models, New York bags, postcards, or just about anything New York themed. Check out the historic flatiron building on your way out! 206 5th Ave., New York, NY 10010; (212) 252-0030; memoriesofnewyork.com.

New York Transit Museum Gallery Annex & Store

There are exhibits and all MTA memorabilia for the Brooklyn museum in Grand Central Terminal. Here's the place for subway flip-flops! Grand Central Terminal, 89 E. 42nd St., New York, NY 10017; (212) 878-0106; grandcentralterminal .com/store/new-york-transit-museum-gallery-annex-and-store/2137026154 /2138781576.

City Store

The city's official shop for all things Big Apple, ranging from socks to official horseshoes from NYPD horses. It's located in the Municipal Building, the impressive domed building downtown that's often mistaken for City Hall next door. Fun fact: When people want to get married at City Hall, they actually have to go to the City Clerk's office in the Municipal Building to do it. Manhattan Municipal Building, One Centre Street, North Plaza, New York, NY 10007; a856-citystore.nyc.gov.

Phantom of Broadway

Here you'll find I Love NY, NYPD, FDNY, Wall Street Bull, and more souvenirs. 1607 Broadway in the Crowne Plaza Hotel; (212) 956-2391; phantomofbroadway.com.

Grand Slam

For Yankees and other Major League Baseball gear as well as other NYC souvenirs. 1557 Broadway, New York, NY; (888) 395-0515; grandslamnewyork.com.

Souvenir Smarts

A lot of kids like to get sports gear from NYC teams when they visit. Whatever you decide to buy:

- Shop smart! Talk to your parents about how much you can spend. Some families save loose change in a big jar to use for vacation souvenirs. It can really add up!

- Decide if you want to use your money for one big souvenir or several smaller ones.

- Resist impulse buys and think about choosing something you can only get in NYC.

- Start a collection! Buy stickers for your water bottle. Collect pins, patches, or keychains to put on your backpack.

What collection could you start?

Chelsea Piers—Come and Play!

If you're in New York and you're looking for a great place to take part in some sports, instead of just watching them, **Chelsea Piers Sports and Entertainment Complex** (chelseapiers.com) is the perfect place to head! Located between 17th and 23rd Streets along the Hudson River, Chelsea Piers contains a golf club, a sports center, a sky rink (ice rink), a field house, a roller rink, and a bowling alley. If you head on over to Chelsea Piers, you can take part in about any sport you can imagine, such as baseball, basketball, bowling, dancing, golf, gymnastics, ice hockey, ice-skating, in-line skating, rock climbing, roller hockey, skateboarding and BMX, and soccer. It's definitely a great place to meet other kids just like you and have lots of fun!

6
Grab the Smartphone & Camera

Where can you go in the middle

of New York City and see five states? The Empire State Building, of course.

But maybe you'd rather ascend to the top of the tallest building in the Western Hemisphere—The One World Observatory downtown at One World Trade Center, 285 Fulton St. New York, NY 10007; (844) 6966-1776; oneworld observatory.com. Hear the stories of those who built this amazing building; step into the Sky Portal—a circular disc that promises to offer an unforgettable view. At City Pulse, there will be HD video monitors where you can get close-up views of the landmarks and neighborhoods below. You can even get something to eat! Ready to ride one of the fastest elevators in the world?

On a clear day you can see New Jersey, Connecticut, Pennsylvania, Massachusetts, as well as New York, from the Observatory on the 86th floor.

Of course New Yorkers still love the Empire State Building. It's one of the most recognizable of New York City's buildings. Everyone looks forward to seeing the colored lights on the Empire State Building from far away too—green for St. Patrick's Day; red, white, and blue for Independence Day; red and green for the holiday season; among others.

Be prepared to wait in line! Many people make the **Empire State Building** (350 Fifth Ave. between 33rd and

34th Streets; esbny.com) one of their must-see stops in New York. More than 100 million people have visited the top of the building. Some people even get married here.

You'll probably see parents and kids from lots of different countries at both places. When you enter One World Observatory's Global Welcome Center, there are greetings in many languages and a special map highlighting visitor's hometowns.

In case you're wondering, the Empire State Building does get hit by lightning, about 100 times a year. It was designed to serve as a lightning rod for the surrounding area. When lightning strikes the tip of the Empire State Building, it travels directly—and harmlessly—down a metal conduit into the ground.

DID YOU KNOW?

The **Empire State Building** was built in just one year, winning the race (with the Chrysler Building) to be the world's tallest building at the time. The building is 1,453 feet, 8⁹⁄₁₆ inches tall.

One World Trade Center is 1,776 feet tall. It takes less than 60 seconds to get to the **One World Trade Center Observatory** on the 100th floor. Many believe that this building symbolizes NYC's strength and pride.

Need some exercise? There's a race up the 1,575 steps from the lobby to the 86th floor of the Empire State Building. Some runners have done it in just 10 minutes.

Wherever you check out the view, it's guaranteed to be an experience you'll want to remember. Ready for a selfie?

Another way to see all of New York's buildings is to sail around them—on a **Circle Line Tour** (Pier 83, W. 42nd Street; 212-563-3200; circleline42.com). Some tours around Manhattan Island take three hours and will give you plenty of opportunities to take pictures of the Statue of Liberty, the skyline, and the Brooklyn Bridge. There's a much shorter high-speed trip running from May to October kids like on *The Beast* where you race by all the skyscrapers (nytours.us). You've got to be 40" tall to ride. Ready for some more cool buildings? Stop in at the **Chrysler Building** (405 Lexington Ave.). The old-fashioned, art deco lobby is worth a stop because there aren't many like it. When Walter Chrysler built his skyscraper in 1930, he wanted the company's headquarters to make people think about his cars. The spire on top looks like a car radiator grille. There are decorations throughout the building that look like old-fashioned hood ornaments, wheels, and cars. Don't miss all the weird gargoyles on the building. There are even transportation scenes painted on the ceiling. How many can you find?

Stop in at **Grand Central Terminal** (42nd Street at Park Ave.; grandcentralterminal.com) while you're nearby. It's been a landmark since 1913. Half a million commuters use this terminal every day. It's a "terminal," not a "station," because every train begins or ends its journey here. See the clock at the central information area? It's got four faces. A lot of kids like to stop in Grand Central to get a snack (head downstairs to the big food court where you'll find food from around the world) and then look at the blue ceiling upstairs. It's a

DID YOU KNOW?

The Radio City Rockettes have been kicking up their heels in their world-famous chorus lines at **Radio City Music Hall** for more than 70 years (1260 Avenue of the Americas; radiocity .com). Since they started, more than 3,000 women have been Rockettes. The women all look like they're the same height, but it's an illusion. The tallest women are at the center with the shortest at either end. Besides performing in the Radio City Christmas spectacular, the Rockettes perform at the tree lighting ceremony at Rockefeller Center, during Macy's Thanksgiving Day Parade, and even the presidential inauguration.

painting of more than 2,500 stars. How many constellations can you find? Tip: Little lights pinpoint them.

Quick! Think of a place in New York City where you can see your favorite music star, hear a gigantic dinosaur roar, or catch the latest news.

Stumped? Head directly to **Times Square.** At 42nd Street and Broadway, this is one of the easiest places in New York to reach by public transport since so many bus and subway lines stop here.

New York City kids like to come here because there's so much to do and see in just a few blocks. When your parents were kids, this part of town was so run down that families didn't like to walk around here much. The city has worked hard to clean up and rebuild Times Square in the last 15 years, and now it's usually the first place kids like to come when they visit New York! A lot of people say it's like a city theme park with cool restaurants, big stores,

A VISITING KID SAYS:
"Make sure to go to Times Square and see all the lights. We went to see *The Lion King* and it was so much better than the movie."
—Jessie, 9, Boston, MA

theaters, and even the world's largest TV screen. There are 12,500 hotel rooms here—one-fifth of all the rooms in the city—and more than 250 restaurants.

DID YOU KNOW?

More than eight million people have seen *Hamilton* on Broadway and on tour around the country. Millions more have seen it on Disney+. *Hamilton: An American Musical* is the sung, rap musical by Lin-Manuel Miranda that tells the story of Alexander Hamilton, one of the Founding Fathers. He lived much of his life in New York, the first national capital of the United States.

Kids' Night on Broadway (kidsnightonbroadway.com) is an annual event in New York City during which kids 18 and younger can see a Broadway show free when accompanied by a paying adult. There are also events around the country.

Times Square Scavenger Hunt: Can you find these things on your visit to Times Square?

❑ Hot pretzel

❑ TKTS Booth selling Broadway tickets

❑ A tourist with a camera

❑ The theater where *Hamilton* is playing

❑ The latest news flash

❑ An "I ♥ NY" T-shirt

Music Around the World

Anywhere you go in the city, you are bound to find it:
New York is home to some of the greatest orchestras,
operas, and ballet companies in the world. They
welcome families with special performances just for
them all through the year. You will also hear musicians playing
on street corners and in the subways.

- **Carnegie Hall** (57th Street and Seventh Avenue;
  212-247-7800; carnegiehall.org) has special family
  concerts as well as performances by young musicians.

- The **New York Philharmonic's Young People's Concerts** (nyphil.org/education/family-programs/ypc-family)
  are a series of symphonic performances, old and new, that
  bring kids together.

- **Chamber Music Society of Lincoln Center** has a
  "Meet the Music!" series for kids and their families
  (chambermusicsociety.org/watch-and-listen/playlists/
  meet-the-music).

- **American Ballet Theater** (abt.org) offers the ABT-
  KIDS program, special one-hour performances, and
  certain Pre-Performance workshops in summer.

- The **NYC Ballet** (nycballet.com) offers some interactive
  Family Saturdays with presentations for families, featuring
  short works and excerpts from their repertory. At the

holidays, many families make it a tradition to see the ballet's *Nutcracker* featuring many local children.

- The **Brooklyn Academy of Music** (bam.org) has family workshops and concerts.

- The **Metropolitan Opera** (metopera.org) has special kid-friendly performances of pieces like *Hansel and Gretel* and Mozart's *Magic Flute* at Lincoln Center.

Festival Fever

Whenever you visit, there's a good chance there is some kind of festival, parade, or event that brings out the crowds:

January (or February)—**Chinese New Year** with parades and special feasts in Chinatown

March—**St. Patrick's Day Parade**, the biggest of all the city's parades

April—**Easter Day Parade** on Fifth Avenue with all kinds of crazy hats

May—**Martin Luther King Memorial Day Parade**

June—**Puerto Rican Day Parade**

July—**Independence Day Celebration**

September—**Feast Of St. Gennaro** along Little Italy's Mulberry Street with all kinds of good eats

November—**The New York Marathon** and **Macy's Thanksgiving Day Parade**

December—The dropping of the giant ball in Times Square to celebrate the New Year at midnight, Dec. 31

Check out all the giant signs! Some are huge advertisements, but you can also read the latest news lit up on a moving stripe at One Times Square. Since the late 19th century, this has been the center of the country's theater world. And you can buy souvenirs from the street vendors or in one of the dozens of stores that line the streets.

Check out **Madame Tussaud's New York Wax Museum** (234 West 42nd St.; 866-841-3505; nycwax.com), where you can "meet" Abraham Lincoln, Pharrell Williams,and Carmelo Anthony, among nearly 200 of their friends. Just one thing—they're all made of wax. It's not easy to pose for a wax portrait. Madame Tussaud's sculptors have to take lots of pictures and more than 250 measurements of each body. The sculptor models a clay portrait, and then the clay is molded in plaster. From that mold, the body is cast in fiberglass and the head from wax. Each pair of eyes is made individually— with hand-painted eyeballs

{ **What's Cool?** The New York Philharmonic's online Kidzone: nyphil.org/education/young-peoples-concerts/kidzone-online-learning

to match the real ones. Hair color is perfectly matched to a sample given by the celebrity and each strand is inserted one by one. The same goes with teeth. It takes five weeks just to make a head—six months to create the portrait. And every day, two teams inspect each figure to see if they need any "help" before the museum opens. They regularly get their hair washed and their makeup touched up! The celebrities often donate their own clothes and shoes, so the portraits will look more real. Got your camera? You can pose for a picture with your favorite star. They look so authentic your friends might be fooled. Tip: If you whisper in J-Lo's ear, she blushes!

While you're on 42nd Street, peek inside **Disney's New Amsterdam Theater** (214 W. 42nd St.; theater.disney.go .com/faq.html) a few steps west of Times Square. It's the city's oldest Broadway theater, having opened in 1903, long before your grandparents were born! And it's been completely restored. This is where *The Lion King* opened on Broadway and is still playing to huge crowds.

If you love theater, you will want to visit the new **Museum of Broadway** in the heart of Times Square (145 W 45th St.; themuseumofbroadway.com).

You can visit all the little shops and street vendors selling "I ♥ NY" T-shirts, NYPD and NYFD hats, and replicas and key chains of the Statue of Liberty. What souvenir will you want to take home?

Lots of families like to see a play when they're in New City. You might get to go to one of the big Broadway theaters, or even see what is called an Off-Broadway play. That means it's a smaller, less glitzy production, shown someplace other than the big Broadway theaters. Tickets usually are cheaper too. Would you like to be an actor? Sometimes kids have parts in Broadway productions. They still have to go to school and do their homework, maybe in between their scenes. Sometimes they'll even move to New York City with their mom or dad temporarily to appear in a play. When they graduate from school, a lot of young people come to New York to audition for roles on Broadway. Many also work in restaurants as waiters or waitresses. Next time you're out at a restaurant, ask your server if he or she is an actor!

Sightseeing Smarts

New York is so big, and there's so much to do! You can't see it all. Here's how to have fun sightseeing:

Wear comfortable shoes.

Look at a map or program one into your phone so you know where you're going. (You can get a map at your hotel.)

Stash some snacks and a camera in your pocket.

Alternate sites you want to see like a museum or the Empire State Building with some people-watching, time in the park, or time out for a meal. That way you won't get so tired!

When you get really tired, take a break. You can go to a playground (there are more than 200 in the city!), get something to eat, or go back to the hotel and chill.

Alternate what you want to do and what your parents want you to see. That way everybody gets to lead the pack—some of the time.

Holiday Glitter

You've probably seen it on TV. There's been a big Christmas tree in front of **Rockefeller Center** (rockefellercenter .com) since 1931! A special team goes all around the East Coast looking for the perfect tree. The Rockefeller Center Tree starts in someone's backyard where it's been growing for years and years. When asked, families donate the tree, which is then carefully brought into NYC with a police escort on a custom-made trailer. It takes at least 15 people and a 280-ton crane to handle the tree. More than 26,000 light-emitting diodes and five miles of wire decorate the tree. The same star has been used on top for more than 50 years. It's 5 feet wide! Of course the tree can be 100 feet tall. After the holidays, the tree is ground into mulch and used in the city's parks.

A VISITING KID SAYS:
"In the winter, it's really fun to go ice-skating at Rockefeller Center."
—Shelby, 9, NJ

Circus!

New York kids love the circus as much as kids everywhere. If you're visiting in the fall or winter, you might want to see the **Big Apple Circus,** the one-ring circus under a Big Top tent that's become a holiday tradition for New York families (Damrosch Park at Lincoln Center, 150 West 65th Street, NYC 800-922-3772; bigapplecircus.com). There are acrobats, jugglers, dogs, clowns, flying trapeze artists, and more.

The United Nations

The **United Nations Building** (First Avenue between 42nd and 46th Streets; un.org) towers over the East River and is another must-see site. Your parents definitely will think so. The UN is the voluntary organization that countries around the world have joined to help keep peace, to develop friendlier relations among different countries, and to help poor people live better. Maybe you've collected pennies for UNICEF at Halloween time. That is a United Nations effort. Certainly you've heard about UN peacekeeping troops being sent to different countries around the world. Take a guided tour. You'll learn a lot about the work the delegates and staff do here as well as about the building. Have you ever seen so many people from so many different countries in one building?

DID YOU KNOW?

The pair of marble lions that stands outside the **New York Public Library** at Fifth Avenue and 42nd Street has been welcoming New Yorkers since the library opened in 1911 (nypl.org). First they were called Leo Astor and Leo Lenox, after New York Public Library founders John Jacob Astor and James Lenox. But during the 1930s, Mayor Fiorello La Guardia dubbed them Patience and Fortitude, for the qualities he thought New Yorkers needed to survive the Great Depression. And these names have stuck. Patience is on the south side of the steps and Fortitude on the north. If you visit at holiday time, they might have giant wreaths around their necks.

{ **What's Cool?** All of the lights in Times Square at night.

7

Lady Liberty &
Ellis Island

The Statue of Liberty

was a thank-you gift from France to the US that took more than 20 years to arrive.

And when she did come, she was packed in 214 crates, like a giant jigsaw puzzle that had to be put together. Good thing they sent directions along too.

A VISITING KID SAYS:
"I never really knew how big the Statue of Liberty is. And I like the boat ride to get there."
—Joey, 12, Chicago, IL

DID YOU KNOW?

The Statue of Liberty is green because it's made of copper and copper oxidizes when exposed to the air. It took 30 years for the statue to turn green!

When you're visiting the **Statue of Liberty** and **Ellis Island,** you're visiting a national park (nps.gov/stli). You can become a Junior Ranger at the Statue of Liberty or Ellis Island. Web Rangers is an online extension of the Junior Ranger program (nos.gov/webrangers).

You won't want to miss the Statue of Liberty Museum on Liberty Island with its interactive galleries, including the multimedia experience. Ready to virtually fly through the Inside of Lady Liberty? You also will be able to explore what took place in sculptor Frédéric Auguste Bartholdi's studio. Add your own self portrait to the digital collage called "Becoming Liberty."

But what a present the Statue of Liberty turned out to be! Originally planned as a gift of the people of France to the people of the US to commemorate their long friendship, she stands in New York Harbor as the most famous symbol of liberty and freedom in the world. She's also the biggest metal statue ever constructed.

Immigrants cried when they saw her because they knew their long sea voyage was over. Today, a lot of people get choked up when they see Lady Liberty all lit up for the first time.

To get to the Statue of Liberty, you ride a ferry (877-523-9849; statue cruises.com) from Battery Park across New York Harbor to Liberty Island. It takes about 15 minutes, and then you can get back on the same ferry to visit Ellis Island.

The original idea was that the French people would build the statue and transport it to the US. The Americans were supposed to build the pedestal on which she would stand. The French raised the money they needed. But in the US, no one seemed to want to give any money to help. Finally, the *New York World,* a 19th-century newspaper, launched a big campaign to raise the needed funds.

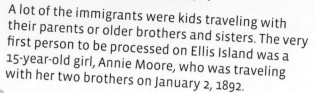

Even schoolkids contributed. People all around the country started to send money, and just before the statue arrived in 1885, enough money had been raised to build the pedestal. She was unveiled the next year, in October 1886.

The sculptor Frédéric Auguste Bartholdi used his mom as the model for the Statue of Liberty's face. He spent more than 20 years on the project and put a lot of symbols into her. For example, the seven rays of her crown are supposed to represent the seven seas and the seven continents. The tablet she holds is engraved with the date of American independence, July IV, MDCCLXXVI (July 4, 1776), and her torch means she's lighting the way to freedom and liberty. At her feet are chains to symbolize her escaping the chains of tyranny.

On the second floor of the Statue Pedestal, you can see replicas of the statue's face and foot. They are big! And just think of the work it took to create this colossal statue.

She's made of copper sheets with an iron framework. It wasn't easy. The framework was designed and built by Gustave Eiffel, the great French engineer who later built the Eiffel Tower.

ELLIS ISLAND

Ellis Island is north of Liberty Island, about a 10- to 15-minute ferry ride on the Circle Line-Statue of Liberty Ferry from Battery Park. Maybe someone in your family arrived in the US here. Before 1892, individual states oversaw immigration, but as the numbers of immigrants increased, it got to be too big of a job.

The Great Hall, where the immigrants waited when they arrived on Ellis Island, is part of the museum. Look around. Do you think you would have been scared, not speaking the language, wearing clothes that looked different? Probably you would have been hungry and possibly sick after two weeks on a rocking boat.

Between 1892 and 1954, 12 million immigrants passed through Ellis Island. Each one had to pass a six-second

A VISITING KID SAYS:
"The way New York looked from the boat going to see the Statue of Liberty was really cool!"
—Brandon, 9, Los Angeles, CA

medical exam in the Great Hall before they could enter the US to see if they had any of 60 different diseases like diphtheria, measles, or any other contagious illness or disability that would keep them from being able to earn a living. Ninety-eight percent passed.

It's important to remember that everyone who came to the US in those days didn't have to come through Ellis Island—not if they had more money. "Steerage," or third-class, passengers were the ones who landed here after upward of two weeks on crowded ships where they faced rough seas without much chance to get any fresh air.

DID YOU KNOW?

Over 100 million Americans trace their ancestry to those immigrants who passed through Ellis Island. Many immigrants still come to New York in search of a better life. People here in New York City come from nearly 200 different countries. You can search over 65 million immigrant arrival records If you think a relative might have come through Ellis Island. Start at www.statueofliberty.org.

What's Cool? Visiting the **Lower East Side Tenement Museum** (108 Orchard St.; 212-982-8420; tenement.org), where you see what it was like for the immigrant families who lived and often worked in these tiny apartments. The museum is housed in an old tenement apartment building. Imagine going down four flights of steps to go to the bathroom outside!

When you visit Ellis Island, you can watch a movie about the immigrants who came here. Sometimes, professional actors bring to life the stories that immigrants have told over the years. Check when you arrive to see what time these plays start.

You might also get to see the reenactment of an immigrant hearing, just as it would have been conducted to determine whether the immigrant could stay in the US. Some of the exhibits might not be open, however.

Make sure to stop at the American Immigrant Wall of Honor, just outside the "peopling of America" exhibit. The

What's Cool? Going to the top of the Statue of Liberty pedestal—the top of the pedestal is roughly half the height of the entire monument. There is no additional fee for the pedestal. You'll need advance reservations along with your ferry tickets (cityexperiences.com/new-york/city-cruises/statue).

wall is inscribed with more than 600,000 names of those who came through Ellis Island. Families have paid to have their immigrant relative's names engraved.

You can really understand looking at all those different names from all those different countries and cultures why people call this country a melting pot. Your own family probably is one too. How many different countries do your relatives come from?

A lot of kids who come to NYC try food they haven't eaten at home. Check off what you've tried:

- ❏ a hot dog from a street vendor
- ❏ a hot salted pretzel or roasted nuts from a street vendor
- ❏ a slice of NYC pizza folded in half (that's the way New Yorkers eat it)
- ❏ a pastrami sandwich
- ❏ a fresh bagel with a shmear (of cream cheese)
- ❏ Chinatown noodles or rice with chopsticks

{ **What's Cool?** Trying a kind of food you've never tasted.

- If you come from a family of immigrants, you can look up a relative and their history on the huge electronic database at the American Family Immigration History Center here. (Start online at statueofliberty.org/ellis-island.) Over 12 million immigrants came through Ellis Island from 1892 to 1924 when Ellis Island was the largest immigration station in the country.

- Before you come, gather as much information as you can, including first and last names, ethnicity and religion, approximate age on arrival, the ship, port of departure, and whether your relative was traveling with anyone else. If you find your relative's name, you can keep copies of the passenger records and chip images in a profile you can open by registering on Ellis Island, and you can purchase reproductions.

Grab a tape measure!

The height from the foot of the Statue of Liberty to the tip of the flame is 151 feet, 1 inch (from the ground, 305 feet, 1 inch). She weighs 225 tons (445,000 pounds).

She's one big lady!

Her index finger: 8 feet

Her head: 17 feet, 3 inches

Nose: 4 feet

Right arm: 42 feet

Mouth: 3 feet wide (when she's not smiling)

A VISITING KID SAYS:
"Get a Statue of Liberty foam crown."
—John, 8, Greensboro, NC

DID YOU KNOW?

It's 354 steps from the entrance to the crown of the Statue of Liberty.

You get a terrific view of the Statue of Liberty on the free Staten Island Ferry across New York Harbor.

You've probably heard some of these words: "Give me your tired, your poor, your huddled masses yearning to breathe free." They're part of a very famous poem written in 1883 by Emma Lazarus. You can read the entire poem on a plaque in the statue museum.

Becoming a Citizen

The US is often called a melting pot or salad bowl because so many immigrants have come here from different countries and cultures looking for a better life. Many children whose parents are immigrants are citizens because they were born here. But just living here doesn't automatically make you a citizen. If you've come to the US from another country, to become a citizen you must:

- Be at least 18.

- Live in the US for five years or more.

- Be of good moral character and loyal to the US.

- Be able to read, write, and speak basic English to pass a test.

- Have enough basic knowledge of the US government and history to pass a test.

- Be willing to take an oath of allegiance to the US.

Once you've filed all the necessary documents and passed the tests, you appear before a judge and ask to become a citizen. You take a special oath. It's a very exciting day. Many immigrants live in the US their whole lives without becoming citizens.

Staying Safe on Vacation

Write down the name and phone number of the hotel where you're staying or put it in your phone. Make sure you have your parents' numbers too.

Practice "what if" situations with your parents. What should you do if you get lost in a museum? On a city street?

Decide when you arrive at a tourist destination on a central easy-to-locate spot.

If you get separated from your parents, only ask uniformed people for help—police officers, firefighters, store security guards or clerks, museum officials wearing official badges.

Pack Your Trunk!

When immigrants came in the last century, there was no e-mail, no TV, no Instagram or YouTube, and most people didn't have telephones. The only way to find out more about life in America was by writing a letter to a relative already here. Sometimes, they exchanged photos so they'd know whom to look for when they arrived. Some teenagers came by themselves. If you were coming to America, you could only bring one small trunk with 30 things. You may be able to see some of what immigrants chose to bring with them in the Treasures from Home exhibit on the third floor of the museum on Ellis Island. What would you bring with you? Make a list on the next page!

What's Cool? Walking around the Lower East Side and seeing what bargains you can find from the street vendors.

I would bring . . .

1. _____
2. _____
3. _____
4. _____
5. _____
6. _____
7. _____
8. _____
9. _____
10. _____
11. _____
12. _____
13. _____
14. _____
15. _____
16. _____
17. _____
18. _____
19. _____
20. _____

Who's in your family?
Draw your family tree here.

8

Yummy Foods, Giant Balloons & Bargains

Grab your chopsticks!

Everyone who comes to New York for
the first time should have dinner in
Chinatown. With the Chinese lanterns
and telephone booths, and everyone
speaking Chinese, it's like stepping
into a Chinese city right in downtown
New York. There are hundreds of restaurants to choose from.

You can also explore different cultures if you venture
out of Manhattan. Some neighborhoods are known for the
food of those who live there. Besides Little Italy, you will
find Italian food on Arthur Avenue In the Bronx; Astoria
in Queens is known for its Greek community and Greek
restaurants and shops. Flushing, Queens, is sometimes
called the "Chinese Manhattan." Jackson Heights,
Queens, is home to many South Asians and a good place
to try Indian dishes.

A NYC KID SAYS:
"I love eating in Chinatown. Try the
pork or the crab, and if you pay
attention, you can even learn how to
use chopsticks!"
—Laurel, 11, Queens, NY

A NYC KID SAYS:
"There is this amazing candy shop called Dylan's Candy Bar. Every kid needs to try it!"
—Jason, 12, NYC

You'll hear more Chinese spoken than English here in Lower Manhattan just south of Canal Street and a short walk from the Lower East Side. Even the street signs are in Chinese.

Browse in stores along Mott Street that sell Chinese toys, herbs, and all kinds of strange-looking foods. If you want to learn more about the history of Chinatown and the people who settled here, stop in at the **Museum**

{ **What's Cool?** Counting how many different buses you've been on while in NYC. There are 4,373 buses, the world's largest fleet of buses, serving over 666 million people a year!

of Chinese in America (215 Centre St.; 212-619-4785; mocanyc.org).

Of course you're going to eat. The restaurants here are big—and tiny. Sometimes, the waiters don't speak English, but the menus often are printed in Chinese and English. Any kind of noodle dish is a good bet, New York kids say.

DID YOU KNOW?

You can learn the stories of those who labored in the tunnels more than 100 years ago to build the subway system at the **New York Transit Museum** in Brooklyn (130 Livingston St.). It is the largest museum in the country devoted to urban public transportation. There are virtual programs and more information at nytransitmuseum.org.

A NYC KID SAYS:
"When you come to Little Italy, you should look around at the decorations in the streets. But what you have to do most is eat! I love it here."
—Nicholas, 9, NYC

They also like to come here on weekends for the Chinese brunch called dim sum. You pick all kinds of little dumplings from carts the waiters roll around the restaurant.

Little Italy is another old-fashioned neighborhood that's a favorite with kids and parents. It's just north of Canal Street and Chinatown. You'll find lots of little restaurants here too where you can have pizza, pasta, lasagna, and yummy Italian pastries and ice cream. Some families like to go to Chinatown for dinner and Little Italy for dessert. If you're visiting in September, all of Mulberry Street becomes a huge outdoor restaurant at the Festival of San Gennaro.

Of course you can get any kind of food you want in New York from an omelet in Greenwich Village to burgers in Midtown.

Kids like **American Girl Place** (75 Rockefeller Plaza; 877-247-5223; americangirl.com), where they come for tea or lunch at the cafe where their dolls get VIP treatment too and are served on special tiny china while sitting on doll-size seats. And everyone likes the loud, friendly **Carmine's** (200 West 44th Street New York, NY 10036; 212-221-3800; carminesnyc.com/locations/

times-square), a restaurant serving family style platters of delicious southern Italian food.

Kids think these stores are fun because they're like being in a giant treasure chest. Girls can try on makeup and perfume; boys can sample food.

There's lots of special NYC gear too.

There are lots of other stores in NYC too—big ones and small ones. Even museums have great stores in New York. It's fun just to window-shop—and people-watch everywhere.

Don't forget your birthday money.

{ **What's Cool?** Eating a "a slice" of pizza New York-style—folded in half.

Macy's Thanksgiving Day Parade

Camels and elephants were part of the first Macy's Parade held on Thanksgiving Day 1924. Horses pulled the floats!

Today, of course, the entire world watches the parade on TV, and millions of parents and kids line the route in New York City. There are bands—they compete from all over the country to get a spot— clowns, floats, singers, dancers including the Radio City Rockettes, and, of course, the giant balloons.

A NYC KID SAYS:
"If you go to the Macy's Thanksgiving Parade, wear a lot of layers. It gets freezing!"
—Ronni, 9, NYC

The balloons have been a Macy's Parade tradition since 1927. In fact, to blow up the giant balloons Macy's uses more helium than anyone else in the country except the US government. A team of 10 artists works on designing and building the balloons all year long.

A lot of NYC kids like to go watch the balloons getting inflated the night before the Macy's Thanksgiving Day Parade. The balloons are rolled out and anchored with sandbags to keep them from flying away. (Hint: go to West 77th and 81st Streets between Columbus and Central Park West between 3 and 10 p.m.) The balloon lineup takes up two full city blocks.

TELL THE ADULTS:

Kids don't want to be limited to kids' menus, and you don't want them eating a steady diet of chicken fingers, fries, and mac and cheese on vacation. Vacation is a great time to try new foods, and it's not too hard to eat healthy along the way.

A NYC KID SAYS:
"Take the subway when you're in a hurry. They're the quickest and buses are slower."
—Sarah, 9, NYC

1. Get the kids thinking about vacation as an adventure for their taste buds as much as a chance to explore new places. Let them pick the kind of food they want for dinner! You can search by the kind of food, price, or location on websites like yelp.com/c/nyc/restaurants.

2. Suggest that rather than ordering from the kids' menu, the kids order an appetizer or half portion from the regular menu.

3. Visit a farmers' market. There are more than 50 to choose from in New York, with over 230 family farms and fishermen participating. Especially in summer, you can find markets all around the city and buy what you need for a picnic in a park. Check out grownyc.org/greenmarket/ourmarkets.

A VISITING KID SAYS:
"I went shopping at Macys and it's huge and I loved it!"
—Victoria, 15, Sydney, Australia

4. Stash healthy snacks in your backpack.

Good Eats

FOR BBQ—**Virgil's Real Barbeque** near Times
Square (152 W. 44th St., New York, NY 10036;
virgilsbbq.com; second location on the Upper
West Side)

FOR PIZZA—**John's Pizzeria** (260 W. 44th St.,
New York, NY 10036; 212-391-7560;
278 Bleeker St; johnspizzerianyc.com)

FOR CHINESE—**Chinatown**
(explorechinatown.com), west
of the Bowery and south of
Canal Street

FOR MAC AND CHEESE—
Bubby's, which has plenty else
on the menu (120 Hudson St.,
New York, NY 10013; 212-219-
0666; bubbys.com)

FOR SINGING AND DANCING WAITERS—**Ellen's
Stardust Diner** just near Times Square (1650
Broadway, New York, NY 10019; 212-956-5151;
ellensstardustdiner.com)

FOR A PLACE EVERYONE CAN GET SOMETHING
DIFFERENT—**Hudson Eats at Brookfield Place**,

with 14 chef-driven eateries, including sushi, ramen, tacos, burgers, and more (230 Vesey St., New York, NY 10282; 212-978-1673; bfplny.com/food)

Midtown on the East Side, **The Hugh**, with everything from Jamaican jerk, kabobs, ramen, Mediterranean and African street food, pizza, burgers, and more (157 East 53rd Street, New York, NY 10022; thehughnyc.com)

FOR BURGERS—**Bareburger**, where you can get an elk burger, quinoa burger, and great grilled cheese and milkshakes. There are lots of locations (535 Laguardia Place, New York, NY 10012; 212-477-8125; bareburger.com). **5 Napkin Burger** is another good choice with several locations (5napkinburger.com).

FOR SUNDAY BRUNCH—**Sarabeth's**, where you should try the french toast! There are a few locations, but this one,

right across from Central Park, is great if you want to see the carriage horses or walk around the park (40 Central Park S, New York, NY 10019; 212-826-5959; sarabeth.com)

FOR DELI—You'll find delis everywhere in NYC, but **Katz's Delicatessen** is the city's oldest (205 E. Houston St., New York, NY 10002; 212-254-2246; katzsdelicatessen.com)

FOR ITALIAN—**Little Italy** (littleitalynyc.com), where you have many restaurants to choose from, and where you'll want to go to **Ferrara** for dessert—Italian pastries and gelato (195 Grand St., New York, NY 10013; 212-226-6150; ferraranyc.com)

FOR THE ONLY NUTELLA BAR IN NYC— **Eataly NYC**, where you might be able to watch an Italian cooking demonstration, shop for a picnic, and take your pick of seven restaurants

(200 Fifth Ave., New York, NY 10010; 212-229-2560; eataly.com)

FOR SWEETS:

Max Brenner New York Chocolate Restaurant—with chocolate pizza, chocolate chunk waffles, chocolate fondue, make your own s'mores, and much more (841 Broadway, New York, NY 10003; 646-467-8803; maxbrenner.com)

Ample Hills Creamery—Local kids think it's the best in the city and the largest ice cream production facility in NYC (305 Nevins St., Brooklyn, NY 11215; 347-725-4061; amplehills.com). More locations in the city.

Economy Candy—Everything from old-fashioned candy shoelaces to Harry Potter's Chocolate Frogs to barrels of every gummy animal (108 Rivington St., New York, NY 10002; 212-254-1531; economycandy.com)

Dominique Ansel Bakery—Try the cronuts or the cookies shaped into a cup with milk inside! (189 Spring St., New York, NY 10012; 212-219-2773; dominiqueansel.com)

Alice's Tea Cup—The most famous order here is the "Mad Hatter," which includes sandwiches, scones, cookies, and, of course, tea (156 East 64th St., New York, NY 10065; 212-486-9200; alicesteacup.com)

Dylan's Candy Bar—Come for chocolate souvenirs! (1011 Third Ave., New York, NY 10065; 646-735-0078, dylanscandybar.com)

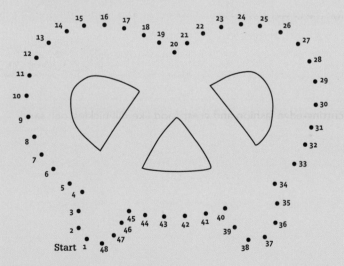

Connect the dots to draw a New York City street food favorite!

Calling All Bargain Lovers

Every Sunday Orchard Street is closed to traffic from Delancey Street to E. Houston Street so merchants can put their merchandise out onto the street like in the old days. (Remember, Houston Street is pronounced, "HOW-ston street" by New Yorkers.)

More than 100 years ago, when immigrant families lived in the tall tenements in Lower Manhattan, peddlers hit the streets selling their wares out of potato sacks. They expanded to pushcarts and eventually store-fronts selling everything from pots and pans to underwear to vegetables. The website for the Lower East Side area of stores and restaurants is lowereastsideny.com.

New Yorkers have always come to Orchard Street and the surrounding neighborhood looking for bargains. Today, they also come for cutting-edge fashion and great food like dill pickles, deli sandwiches, knishes, and more.

You'll still find great bargains on everything from leather jackets to purses to jewelry, perfume, and shoes. Don't be afraid to bargain: the storeowners expect it!

9
Monkeys, Elephants,
Polar Bears &
Alice in Wonderland

Let's have some fun in the sun...

or the snow. It doesn't matter. Central Park is the place New York kids go to play, and you can too.

There's plenty of room for sure. **Central Park** stretches for 50 city blocks between the Upper East and West Sides—843 acres smack in the middle of Manhattan.

It's been here for more than 150 years, since the city paid for a chunk of land that back then was virtually a dump. Today some New Yorkers pay just as much as the city did then for apartments just to overlook the park.

A NYC KID SAYS:
"You should definitely go to the merry-go-round and skate on Wollman Rink at night and go to the zoo— the bears are really cool."
—Chris, 10, NYC

When you get to the park, stop in at **The Dairy** at the south end. In the 1870s, city children could get fresh milk here. Now the Victorian building is the Park Visitor

DID YOU KNOW?

There are 21 different playgrounds in **Central Park** and more than 200 across the city. The websitescentralparknyc.org and nycgovparks.org can steer you to all the city play lots.

The Heckscher Playground is Central Park's oldest, built nearly a century ago , and its biggest, complete with a water play area and climbing maze. Kids love Ancient Playground near the Metropolitan Museum with its pyramid-style climbing structures. Adventure Playground is one of the most unique, including a wood pyramid, and granite climbing mound with tunnel and slide. Of course, there's a water feature too!

Central Park is a great place to meet local kids.

A NYC KID SAYS:
"The best part about Central Park is all the cool shows they have there in the summer. And sometimes my parents take me to those operas on the big lawn. Those are cool because all my friends are there too."
—Kelly, 14, Manhattan

Center and Gift Shop, where you can pick up a map and find out what's happening in the park the day you're there.

Nearby, you'll find the **Wollman Rink** (wollmanskating rink.com), where a lot of kids like to ice-skate in the winter. In the summer the rink is transformed into a little amusement park called **Victorian Gardens** (to get there enter Central Park from 59th Street and Sixth Avenue and walk north; 212-982-2229; victoriangardensnyc.com).

Central Park offers many concerts throughout the summer, and most of them are free. You can see shows ranging from some of your parents' favorite older artists to some of your favorite pop performers! So if you are going to be traveling to NYC in the summertime, you should check to see who is going to be playing in the park when you are there (centralpark.com/guide/activities/concerts.html). Maybe it will be someone you would like to see! Then check out the **Central Park Zoo** (at 64th Street and Fifth Avenue; centralparkzoo.com).

A NYC KID SAYS:
"Every kid who visits NYC should not miss the Central Park Zoo. It's fun to see the animals!"
—Josh, 7, Brooklyn

A VISITING KID SAYS:
"Walk all of the secret paths in Central Park and go watch a concert on the weekend in the summer."
—Toby, 13, Weston, CT

DID YOU KNOW?

There are over 9,000 benches in Central Park. They would stretch 7 miles if placed end to end.

There are 24,000 trees and 250 acres of lawn in Central Park—plenty of places to run around!

You'll love the penguins, sea lions, monkeys, and more. There's even a roaring waterfall and tropical birds.

There's a great playground near the Children's Zoo complete with a 45-foot spiral slide. Don't miss the George Delacorte Musical Clock. It's right near the Children's Zoo, and every hour a nursery rhyme plays while a bear with a tambourine, a hippo with a violin, a goat with panpipes, a kangaroo with horns, and a penguin with a drum glide around the base.

In the middle of the park at West 72nd Street, heading north, you'll pass Strawberry Fields. This is one of the park's most visited spots and was named to honor John Lennon, who lived nearby and could see this spot from his apartment building. It's an international peace garden with plants from every country in the world. Look for the mosaic in the pathway. It's inscribed with IMAGINE to remind people of the message of peace in Lennon's song.

A lot of kids also like to hang out in the **Sheep Meadow.** (Yes, there were sheep here in the park's first years.)

Cross a bridge yet? There are 36 bridges in the park—no two of them alike—and 58 miles of paths where you can walk, run, or ride horses and bikes.

The old-fashioned carousel is in the middle of the park at 64th Street. It's one of the biggest in the whole country!

Keep an eye out for **Alice in Wonderland.** You'll find her along with the Cheshire Cat, the Mad Hatter, and the Dormouse at the northern end of the Conservatory Water where kids and grown-ups like to sail model boats. Try sliding down her toadstool seat!

Kids also like the Hans Christian Andersen statue showing him reading *The Ugly Duckling.* Kids like to climb onto the book—and the duck.

Say hi to **Balto the Dog** (at East 67th Street near the East Drive). Balto was the leader of the husky sled team that carried the serum across Alaska to save people from dying of diphtheria. Bet you didn't think you were going to learn a little history here in the park!

Of course, you'd probably prefer to run around, climb some rocks, or have a picnic under a tree. Where's the Frisbee?

While you're in the park, see if you can find these special things . . .

- ❏ Balto the sled dog
- ❏ Alice in Wonderland
- ❏ Mother Goose
- ❏ The carousel
- ❏ The Dairy
- ❏ A fancy fountain
- ❏ A police officer on a horse
- ❏ Strawberry Fields
- ❏ A bridge

TELL THE ADULTS:

- The Central Park website, centralparknyc.org, can steer you in the right direction. And you can borrow or rent what you need.

- Rent in-line and roller skates at **Wollman Rink** on the East Side between 62nd and 63rd Streets, where you can also rent ice skates and skate in the winter.

- Rent bicycles, even two-seater tandems, at the **Loeb Boathouse** parking lot at East 74th Street, daily from March through October.

- Borrow a basketball to play at the **North Meadow Recreation Center**, mid-park at 97th Street.

- Fish at the **Harlem Meer**, stocked with a wide variety of fish, at the northeast corner of the park.

- Rent a rowboat April through October at the **Loeb Boathouse** (East Side between 74th and 75th Streets) to take out on Central Park's 22-acre lake (thecentralparkboathouse .com).

- Play chess or checkers at the special tables inside the park at 65th Street just west of The Dairy, where you can borrow chess or checker pieces.

- Sail your own model sailboat at **Conservatory Water** (East Side between 72nd and 75th Streets) or call Central Park Sailboats at (917) 796-1382.

- You can also have a picnic and watch the kids climb some rocks.

It Pays to Be Green

Got your reusable water bottle?

It will become a great souvenir when you slap stickers on it from all the places you've visited in New York. And you'll be helping the planet too instead of using disposable plastic water bottles.

You'll be helping the planet too when you take public transportation, walk, or bike in NYC. (The traffic is terrible anyway!)

The Wildlife Conservation Society, which oversees the Central Park Zoo and the Bronx Zoo, among others, sends scientists around the world to help endangered animals and inspire grown-ups and kids alike to value nature (wcs.org).

Here are some other simple things you can do to help the environment while you are in NYC:

- Turn off the lights and the air-conditioning or heat when you leave your hotel room

- Recycle

- Reuse towels

- Take shorter showers

DID YOU KNOW?

More than 200 movies have included scenes in Central Park. Have you seen *Men in Black II, Stuart Little, You've Got Mail,* or *The Muppets Take Manhattan?* Can you name another one?

A VISITING KID SAYS:
"Don't miss the penguins at the Central Park Zoo. There's a good playground there too."
—Alex, 9, Chatham, NJ

What's Cool? The puppet shows at the Swedish Cottage Marionette Theatre at West 79th Street (212-988-9093).

Birdwatching in Central Park. Located along the Atlantic Flyway, Central Park welcomes more than 210 bird species each year. Many birds live in the Park year-round, with others making an important stop in the Park to rest and feed during spring and fall migrations.

The epic granite slide at the Billy Johnson Playground in Central Park.

Play Time!

Even in a city like New York, you can't sightsee all the time! Good thing there are so many playgrounds. And they are all so different (nycgoparks.org).

The Chelsea Waterside Playground in Hudson River Park (181 11th Ave., New York, NY; hudsonriverpark.com) has a multicolored 64-foot wooden slide in the shape of a Pipefish, one of the many fish that live in the park waters (Hudson River Park, W 23rd St., New York, NY 10011).

Imagination Playground at South Street Seaport (158 John Street) gives you the chance to build your own play structures from giant foam blocks (Front St., John St., and South St., New York, NY 10038).

Splash Pad in Prospect Park in Brooklyn with its massive water play area—47 jets of water (at LeFrak Center near the Lincoln Road and Parkside/Ocean Avenue entrances to the Park; prospectpark.org).

Slide Hill on Governors Island has a slide with a three-story drop, the longest in NYC! (910 Half Moon Rd., Brooklyn, NY 11231; www.govisland.com).

Pier 6 Playgrounds at Brooklyn Bridge Park has a Water Lab, Slide Mountain, Sandbox Village, and Swing Valley.

Dinosaur Playground in Riverside Park near the American Museum of Natural History with fiberglass dinos near the slides (6681 Riverside Dr., New York, NY 10027).

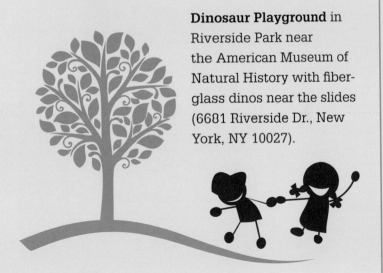

10

The Freedom Tower, One World Observatory, a Memorial & Museum

September 11, 2001 . . .

that's such a long time ago for kids! You weren't even born yet.

But your parents and grandparents certainly remember that awful day. Maybe older siblings, too.

None of us can understand why someone would do something so terrible.

This event changed all of our lives. We realize that every time we stand in a long line and take off our shoes to go through security at airports.

> A NYC KID SAYS:
> "It's hard for kids to understand but 9/11 affects all of us and it is important to know what happened."
> —David, 16, NYC

Now, more than 20 years later, we can go to the 9/11 Memorial and remember and honor those who were killed when terrorists flew planes into the World Trade Center towers.

DID YOU KNOW?

George Washington was inaugurated near the location of the 9/11 Memorial on Wall and National Streets, not in Washington DC. Look for the Federal Hall National Memorial that marks the spot.

{ **What's Cool?** Battery Park located on the southern tip of Manhattan Island facing New York Harbor with great views of the Statue of Liberty.

St. Paul's Chapel, part of the Parish of Trinity Wall Street in Lower Manhattan, became known as "The Little Chapel that Stood," as it is directly across from the World Trade

Center but wasn't damaged. It became a place for volunteers and first responders to rest. Today, tourists from around the world visit. There are memorial banners from around the world here.

DID YOU KNOW?

The **World Trade Center** once included seven buildings. When the World Trade Center was built in 1973, the 110-story Twin Towers became the tallest buildings in the world. Some 50,000 people worked here—more people than live in many suburban towns! Today, the SkyPod Elevators at One World Observatory climb 102 stories In 47 seconds.

What's Cool? The multimedia Horizon Grid highlighting famous faces and places viewable from the One World Observatory. There are 145 screens!

Of the 2,752 people from more than 90 countries who died at the World Trade Center on September 11, 2001, 343 were firefighters.

The **National September 11 Memorial** honors the nearly 3,000 victims who died in the attacks of September 11, 2001, and February 26, 1993. Their names are listed on bronze panels on the memorial.

The design for the memorial was chosen from a competition that included more than 5,000 entrants from 63 nations.

WALLst

Now, we can go to the 9/11 Museum and Memorial and to remember and honor those who were killed and those who worked so tirelessly at the site.

Outside, there are two huge pools sitting in the original footprints of the Twin Towers—each is an acre—with huge waterfalls—the largest manmade waterfalls in the country—surrounding them.

The museum is a serious place but a place

for kids too with drop-in activity stations tied to specific themes in the summer (check the museum's website at 911memorial.org for schedules).

You'll probably see kids from around the world here with their families. Everyone who visits New York wants to pay their respects.

Look at the massive artwork "Trying to Remember the Color of the Sky that September Morning." It's made up of 2,983 squares each painted a unique shade of blue in honor of those killed. See the Survivors' Stairs, one of two outdoor flights that were an escape route. You'll see the mangled Ladder Company 3 Truck, the huge, destroyed elevator motor, and all kinds of artifacts—a firefighter's hat, a shoe, ID cards. There are portraits and histories of those who died. Each person had a family and their own story.

When you get here, you're at the very bottom of Manhattan, the oldest part of New York City and the financial capital of the world. That's one of the reasons why the terrorists chose to attack the Twin Towers.

A VISITING KID SAYS:
"You can't come to the 9/11 Museum and not leave a different person."
—Chris, 15, Westport, CT

The **New York Stock Exchange** (nyse.com) and Wall Street are nearby. Growing numbers of people work here, and more people—including families—live nearby too, as new skyscrapers are being built—most recently **One World Observatory**, the tallest building in the Western Hemisphere.

You can visit the amazing observation deck seven days a week (One World Trade Center, 285 Fulton St., New York, NY 10017; 844-696-1776; oneworldobservatory.com). Tell your parents to get tickets in advance. Once you are at the top, look for the Tour Ambassadors who have interactive presentations that can help you better understand what you are seeing. The special iPads also enable you to get up close to whatever you see from the windows and hear stories about each place. Fun!

Spies Everywhere

George Washington took personal command of the Continental Army at New York in the summer of 1776. Early on, the British troops were successful and occupied the city, making it a political and military center as well as key to Washington's intelligence operation.

After hearing the Declaration of Independence on July 9, 1776, a crowd made its way down Broadway and tore down a large statue of King George III in the center of Bowling Green Park.

When You Visit

Be prepared for security screening, just like at the airport. You can't bring a large backpack or a bag bigger than 8" x 17" x 19", animals (except service animals), glass bottles, skateboards, or weapons.

A VISITING KID SAYS:
"I like thinking about how important it was that people tried to save other people that day. It makes me feel sad, but it's good to come here with your family."
—Jessie, 8, Orlando, FL

DID YOU KNOW?

In 1664, the city's tallest structure was a 2-story windmill!

The Survivor Tree

A Callery pear tree became known as the Survivor Tree after it lived through the September 11, 2001, terror attacks. It was discovered and freed from piles of rubble in the plaza of the World Trade Center and nursed back to health, despite a blackened trunk. It was planted at the memorial in December 2010 and continues to grow among more than 400 swamp white oak trees— an urban forest!

What's Cool? Having a burger in Fraunces Tavern where George Washington told his troops goodbye after the American Revolution was won (54 Pearl St., New York, NY 10024; 212-425-1778; frauncestavernmuseum.org). Check out the museum, which re-creates rooms from that time!

TELL THE ADULTS:

Discussing 9/11 and other senseless terrorist attacks with kids isn't easy. But kids have a lot of questions, whether you visit the 9/11 Memorial and Museum or just hear about yet another terrorist attack on the news. Here is how the 9/11 Memorial experts suggest you start the conversation:

- LISTEN If the kids want to talk about either visiting the museum or their fears, offer them a safe place to share their questions. If they don't want to talk, don't force the discussion.

- DON'T AVOID DIFFICULT CONVERSATIONS It is the attacks themselves that are upsetting, not the conversations. Invite discussion with open-ended questions such as "What would you like to know about 9/11?" Reassure children about their own safety.

- ANSWER QUESTIONS WITH FACTS Children's recollections of 9/11 don't come from their memory, but rather school and the media, among other sources. It is important to answer children's questions with the basic facts.

What a Trip!

I came to New York with:

_____
_____
_____

The weather was:

_____
_____
_____

We went to:

_____
_____
_____

We ate:

_____
_____
_____

We bought:

_____
_____
_____

I saw these famous New York sights:

_____

_____

_____

My favorite thing about New York was:

_____

_____

_____

My best memory of New York was:

_____

_____

_____

My favorite souvenir is:

_____

_____

_____

_____

_____

_____

You had such a great time in New York!!! Draw some pictures or paste in some photos of your trip!!!

Index

```
S T S M U X O M D S D X Y R J E N
T I O A A H E M S N T L W K G T B
A M T N J L S G P Y A B Z A D H R
T E G H R V O W F T V L L W J E O
E S K A Q T H P I W R L S N Z B O
N S H T Z M O E E J I B D I O R K
I Q I T J H L S F V X Y N S N O L
S U E A Z T L R H H R L X R T N Y
L A V N T E K C Z V T G H L R X N
A R E I W K I G R O U N D Z E R O
N E L E X W Z E A F O H R N N X J
D M R E N E D I S M I D T O W N Q
H I H E M C H I N A T O W N E Q U
C T E V L O W E R E A S T S I D E
G R N T R C L W T X N V U H Q W E
G K T D T R I B E C A Q I M X O N
U N S P U O D W K B R N S F B R S
```

145

About the Author

Award-winning author Eileen Ogintz is a leading family travel expert whose syndicated "Taking the Kids" column is the most widely distributed in the country. She has also created TakingtheKids.com, which helps families to make the most of their vacations together. Ogintz is the author of seven family travel books and is often quoted as an expert on family travel in major publications such as *USA Today*, the *Wall Street Journal*, and the *New York Times*, as well as parenting and women's magazines. She has appeared on such television programs as *The Today Show*, *Good Morning America*, and *The Oprah Winfrey Show*, as well as dozens of local radio and television news programs. She has traveled around the world with her family, talking to other traveling families wherever she goes.